INSIDE THE MIND OF *A FLOWER*
Poetry & Journal

INSIDE THE MIND OF A FLOWER
Poetry & Journal

AIYANA FREEMAN

Self-Published by AF the Poet
2019

Copyright © 2019 by Aiyana Freeman

All rights reserved. This book or any portion thereof may not be reproduced or used in any manner whatsoever without the express written permission of the publisher except for the use of brief quotations in a book review or scholarly journal.

First Printing: 2019

ISBN 979-8-9929113-0-5

www.afthepoet.com

DEDICATION

I would love to thank my family for supporting and encouraging me to pursue my passions and dreams. Also, a huge thank you to my close friends and my girls in J.E.T.P.A.D. for being there through it all and sharing life experiences with me.

CONTENTS

Preface ix
I'm Not A Game 1
My Chocolate Isn't Bitter 2
Your Voice 4
Alone 5
Little Black Queen 6
That Place 8
Forgive You 9
Our Angel 10
Let Me Be There 12
Fellas 14
Battles 16
She's Capable 18
Held Hostage 20
Stop Apologizing 22
Will I Ever? 24
Toxicity 26
Black Couples 28
Grown-Ish 30
Shine 33
B&N 33

The Lion King 34

Untitled...Forever 36

Rollercoaster 38

Ode To Poetry 40

My Rock 42

Choose You 44

3 Words 45

Your Privilege 46

No Mj 48

My God 50

Beauty 51

My Anxiety 52

Oblivious 54

Gimme A Minute 56

These Stretch Marks 57

Tunnel Vision 58

Through Your Fingers 60

Middle Man 61

They Can't Make Me Hate You 62

Invasion Of Privacy 64

Reflect Your Thoughts 65

PREFACE

For me, writing poetry was the only way that I could get my thoughts out effectively. Since a little girl, I've seen and heard so many different things that have affected who I am today, and I felt that it was finally time to share all my thoughts with the world. Poetry has given me the opportunity to share my stories along with stories of those around me. My poems are primarily written in first person to give everyone the chance to actually take in the words and translate it to themselves and their life stories. Writing and deciding which poems to place in my book was easy. If the poem still made me feel something, I included it. There was a time a few years ago that I felt I didn't have enough to say, or that my words weren't powerful enough to speak out about. Going through college, I've really learned how to find my voice and found the courage to perform my pieces aloud, for the first time being a pageant for 2017 Miss Phi Beta Sigma Fraternity Inc., and I would like to thank the Illustrious Lambda Iota Chapter for giving me that opportunity. If it weren't for this opportunity, I would have never seen myself performing in front of anyone, ever. I wrote this book to let people have a peek inside the mind of a flower. I used the term flower because my name means "forever flowering", and as I change and grow, I wanted to share what goes through this mind and hopefully it makes you think or gives you the desire to write something yourself, and that is why after the poems I provided a journal section to allow space to release those thoughts.

I'M NOT A GAME

I call BS.
I'm not your PS...
4, The amount of times you had me messed up
Cause your words & actions don't add up
Go back to your X-Box 360
Cause all you did was a 360 with my emotions
We crashed like the ocean
But now the tide is calm
But I still got qualms
About the uncertainty of your mindset
You know your best bet
Stop playing with my mind like a joystick
And figure out your game plan, like Madden
I'm not a Nintendo Game, Boy
I'm not some property or your lil toy
Stepped out my comfort zone
Just for you to press my buttons
And now all of a sudden
It's 2K, I mean 2 A.M.
You created a player
Tailormade for your desire
And I became a supporting character
I rode with the flow,
Tried so hard to press X and let it go
Instead I hit circle & I let you back in
You tried to shoot again...
But... I guess you ran out of credits

MY CHOCOLATE ISN'T BITTER

They say the darker the berry the sweeter the juice
But the lighter the berry the quicker to choose,
And what makes her any different than you?
It's all about perception, and misconceptions
It's about time we get a new perspective.
Black Panther gave dark chocolate a new flavor
Bringing it back & doing us a favor
T'Challa & Nakia
Got me believing Wakanda Foreva
Foreva black & forever beautiful.
But television got us messed up, per usual
Where's the original Aunt Viv & the Angela Bassett's
That dark-skinned beauty full of prowess
And stop making the world believe we're all ratchet.
Teach confidence & self-esteem
Don't need no sugar, don't need no cream...
Cause baby my chocolate isn't bitter.
Just provide roles that makes us better
Now don't get me wrong they need love too, but lack of representation makes it hard to love YOU
To love yourself and all your darkness
Making it hard to believe God made us in his likeness
Look in the mirror and use that reflection
To redirect your thoughts & to get through oppressions
Don't let their words hang you
Don't leave yourself out to dry
Don't strip away your melanin & lose your shine

And yes it's okay to cry, but never lose your glow
Because it's up to society to learn & grow
Stop telling me who I am
Stop portraying this negative light
Stop making me what I'm not
We gon' be alright
Your sun-kissed, dark skin is precious
Love yourself so much it becomes infectious
Standing up for yourself
Isn't downgrading anyone else
So don't tell me to calm down and be sweeter
Cause baby my chocolate isn't bitter.

YOUR VOICE

Sometimes all I wanna hear is your voice
The one that sounds like no other
Now are your responses by choice?
Sometimes I wonder, do you have something to say?
Is it expressed in such a way?
A way we just don't understand
Grab me and take my hand
And express yourself in such a way that everyone can hear
The unspoken words that have been unheard for so long.
The way you talk and how it sounds has gotten lost.
Gotten lost in the past, hoping to be heard in the future.
But since the old has been forgotten, the new must be taught.
Because all I need to hear is your voice again.

ALONE

Feeling alone in this big world
Unable to express your thoughts feeling as though no one knows you're here
But knowing you're always near
Silence in the night, no one awake to talk
Music in your ears, dreaming through the song
Wondering what life is like if that was you
Sitting there, alone
Even though you're at home
No one understands your feelings
And don't know that you're not okay,
Don't care about your day
Or what you have to say
Feeling alone and on your own
Trying to find your way
Sometimes seeing dark clouds
On what really is a bright day
Sitting alone at a table full of people
Feeling like you're sitting around them,
Not with them
Watching, while feeling, alone
On your own
With no one to support you
But you.

LITTLE BLACK QUEEN

Little black girl, look in the mirror
Tell me what you see.

I see, the fear of God looking back at me
I see that beautiful chocolate skin
Kissed from Heaven
Oh yes baby, all that melanin
And the fire in your eyes
Has been there since you were five
Much like, lions and tigers and bears,
"OH MY"
Oh my how you've grown
Into this woman all on her own
With her family by her side
and a man who's down to ride
She was a baby dipped in oils
Filled with the heart of royals
Baby you are a gift from God
Keep walking with your head held high
Feet planted so you can, stand your ground
and please don't let them adjust your crown
Baby girl you are a queen
With the ability to do what others can only dream
When you step into this world
Set your afro free
And tell 'em, "you do you,
and let me do me!"

Now look in the mirror
And tell me what you see
Because I see a little black queen
looking back at me

THAT PLACE

There is always that one
That one place that makes you happy
Or maybe it's an escape; a getaway
An escape from reality
A place where you clear your head
A place to cry and scream
Where no one can hear you
You feel like there's no one to talk to
So you listen to music that makes you cry
Or you sit there and pray asking why?
Why is there so much pain in my heart?
What if you don't know where to start?
Then you start thinking about everything
And it begins to consume you
Your emotions show and you cry
Just thinking about what could have been
Or what may be
Knowing that soon this may become reality.
Escaping to that place
Where emotions are expressed in your face
You stay there 'til you can't cry anymore
Then you face reality
And put on this smile for people to see
Knowing that you are trying to hide
All the pain you feel inside

FORGIVE YOU

I forgive you.
I forgive you but I don't forget you.
Don't forget what you did and the pain it caused.
But I forgive you
See forgiving you doesn't mean trusting you
Because I don't trust you
Don't trust that you won't make the same mistake again
You can beg, you can plead
But the pain I feel will never end
And yes, I forgive you
See, forgiving you is for us
Moving past and moving forward.

Unfortunately, as soon as we move forward
You threw me two steps back
I don't trust you, but I forgave you
That time you didn't ask for it
I gave it to you, for me.
To stop the worry and the panic
To get past all of the antics.
There's nothing you can do, but just know,
I forgive you.

OUR ANGEL

Sunrise and sunset.
At least, that's what it says.
But that doesn't mean the sun always shined.
Dark clouds filled the sky in 2005,
when you attempted, to take your life.
But see, that only dimmed your light.
Spending the last 11 years in a coma,
Forcing the rest of your family to grow closer.
It was April 2016, that brought us all a new beginning.
Our new guardian angel.
That's what you became
The day the Lord called your name.
Taking your soul and leaving flesh behind
Leaving bruises in our hearts, thoughts in our minds
Just wishing, we can turn back the hands of time.
But you left us with memories.
Ones that can only make us laugh and smile.
Maybe shed tears for a little while.
Our new guardian angel,
You gave us the strength and closer we needed,
Even though we may not see it.
Bringing us together to show we care,
And maybe memories we wanted to share.
But now, my new guardian angel,
You've given me a new reason to smile,
Because I can dream.
I can hear that voice and that laugh as we walk down hall

And when you walk in a room that smile is all I saw.
But now, you sit next to the man upstairs.
You're another eye in the sky.
So I make sure to say, "hey Unc" every time I pass by.
Dreams and memories,
Keep our minds at ease.
So keep watching over us,
As we continue to adjust
And amongst the stars you shall twinkle,
Our new guardian angel.

LET ME BE THERE

I consider you a poet, so let me read something
Let me feel your emotions
Let me massage the curves of your back as you write
Watching you ponder all day and into the night to perfect your craft

Let me know what you're thinking
If you need to write through the healing or speak your mind about the community
Baby write about it.

Let me read something
Your emotions are valid and there's no need for you to feel calloused
It's okay.

Let me be your audience.
Baby I'm all ears.
Ready to take in your passions, hear your fights and fears.
Take me through your story
I want to know why you are the man you are today

Let me be your soundboard
As you finetune your words to fit your flow
You have so much to say
Let those words evaporate onto the page and out of the depths of your mind

Let me be your Poetic Justice
The one you can speak your mind too...
Hold or even cry too

Let me be your strong, black woman
The shield protecting her conflicted black man
You don't have to go through this life alone

Let me be your stone
The object that keeps the flood from killing
Or the weight that holds you down when you need her too

No matter what it is you go through
Baby, just let me be there for you

FELLAS

Okaaay King!
Line-up so crisp and clean
Looking geometrically created
Designed and carefully calculated
A look that pierces through my heart
All of you is a piece of art,
Sculpted and precisely cut
Chocolate or chestnut
The richness of your skin is no question
Leaving a lasting impression
Showing up was perfect timing
When my name rolls off your tongue it's mesmerizing
Tantalizing
Always leaving me contemplating
I look at you and see a brotha
Waves on swim
Hair on trim
And that beard...mmm
Conditioned with Shea Moisture
Always doing it for the culture
Out here looking dipped in oil
Body glistenin' like watered soil
You can be 5'10 with sun-kissed skin
Or 6'1 with melanin struck by the sun
It's in the way you carry yourself
It's that look you give that makes me put my attitude on a shelf
Boy, your look gives me butterflies

Those dark brown eyes
And that eye-catching smile
Them cocoa butter kisses
Got me ready to be your Mrs.
King, that swag in your walk, tone of your talk
When your outfit is A1 and you got a fresh cut
That Kenneth Cole Black sprayed on top of that 6-pack
Gives me life
You became intriguing and aesthetically pleasing
Seeing a brotha like this is refreshing
Keep showing off and doing you
Cause baby you're the next GQ.

BATTLES

They say, if you can talk about something without crying, that means you've healed.
What if that's the only way you'll see how I feel?
My tears have a message.
But sometimes I rather choose to suppress it.
When the emotionless show rare emotion they try to protect it.
But, it's okay to not be okay.

Anxiety, hyperventilate...
Stop, breathe, wait.

Let those feelings you're holding in de-escalate.
You're weaker than you look,
Scared to let anyone read you like a book.
Baby the pages are flipping in your mind
And the only thing binding you together is Divine.
Trying to believe all things get better with time,
Cause time heals all wounds
But you can't heal wounds you didn't tend to.
Scars left behind, proving you'll always remember.
Forever have a glimmer of what your past looked like.
A constant battle,
A fight of the mind.
Realizing the difference between emotions is a fine line.
Weighing you down, forcing you to ask why
And the only thing you look to is the sky
Reminding yourself that you're a warrior, so fight

Fight for your self, for your mentality, and life.
Yeah I said life, cause there was a point in time when you were unsure of your actions being right.
Here comes another battle
Do I let them know how I feel, keep it real or lie?
To hold back my words & look you in the eye
And tell you everything's alright
Walking away to cry into the night
Waking up and having to do it all again
Force yourself to smile, put on this fake grin
Spending more time apart,
Trying to see if you could mend your heart
It took a minute but you're over that barrier
And now they say you look happier.
They're glad you found your place
If only they knew the struggle & battles you faced
Glad you overcame, and continued to climb
Stay proactive and nurse your mind.
Your smile was too precious to let fade
Kept praying for better days & God came to your aid
Your happiness is pure now
So look in the mirror and say wow
God did a number on me, but now I have a testimony.

SHE'S CAPABLE

She has the power.
The power to be savage,
Making you forget that one day you had her.
Had her drawn to you and your actions.
For a while she thought you were acting.
But she got to a point when you became average.
Yeah anotha typical, stereotypical brotha...average
And it was that moment when she turned savage
You were that typical person to not add up
Finding holes in your stories, another switch up
Late replies and one too many denies
Forcing her to change her mind
Switch up her mindset
Turning her into something one day you'll regret
2 can play that game
Pointing fingers and placing blame
Telling you she busy
No time to hang
Meanwhile she finding a new man to take your place
And believe she'll go the distance & win this race
Making her willing to go toe to toe
Found a new mentality and a fierce ego
That text you sent at 9 yeah she'll respond at 8
And don't slide back in her DM cause boy you too late
When you ask where she been
She'll tell you with a friend
Meanwhile she holding this man's hand

She was that girlfriend that was worth being a wife
Everything you coulda asked & needed in life
But you took her love for granted
With all your lies & antics
Look back and she wifed up,
All cause you f'd up.
Don't make a good girl go savage
All cause you turned into a dude that became average

HELD HOSTAGE

A fallen king once said:
"Bury me in the ocean with my ancestors that jumped from ships,
because they knew death was better than bondage."
You say you not a slave
You must be lying.
Cause every time I see you, you constantly trying,
Trying to be controlled by your thoughts,
Well maybe it's time for you to get caught.
Cause you a slave to your mentality
Much like captivity
You won't let go of the burdens of your past
Leaving yourself restricted like a cast
People always giving you a way out
Well do like Chris and 'Get Out'
Get out of that destructive mindset
All it's doing is blocking the blessings
Always second guessing, asking what if's
Turn those what if's into did it's
And maybe you stop living a life you regret
Carrying around your problems like a silhouette
Learn to let go, release that degrading ego
You may have daddy issues
And it's okay to,
But that 40 year old bad behavior is a result of bad decisions
Not because of the father you were missing
Stop turning excuses into bruises

To keep from having to grow up and take responsibility for your actions
Cause there will be a time when you are your biggest distraction
Holding yourself hostage
A bondage, a weight you choose to carry
Don't spill your life to social media and not take the criticism
Forever finding a way to turn it into cynicism
No, you put your business out there
Hope somebody will care, lend an ear
Just for you to tell half a story
Waiting for somebody to agree
To help keep you in captivity & incarcerate your intellect
You're only as strong as your weakest link
Well if that link is you mind
Then you've left yourself confined
Shackled to your situations
Constantly longing for negative expectations
Leave your past and struggles where they're at
Stop putting yourself under attack
Break free & get rid of your slave like mentality.
Before it consumes you and causes another casualty.

STOP APOLOGIZING

Stop apologizing for having feelings
Because not being validated forces you to need the healing
Be open and honest, if they can't take it
Welp you could care less, just express it
Start doing more of what makes you happy
Stop apologizing for finding yourself
Making others think they've been put on a shelf
Well if you aren't here for me or supporting my mentality you can go
There's the door
Walk out of it and check yourself before you try to come back in
Cause best believe I don't do well with fake feelings
A smile here, chuckle there, but honestly, do you care
But let me act like I'm listening
You think everything you say is right
Well this is the game of life
And not all things go as planned
You weren't dealt my hand and I always do what I can.
Wear a face mask to preserve my oxygen cause it's wasting
Wasting away on words unheard
I used to talk and feel like nothing was coming out
Because when I had something to say you act like only your thoughts count.
Guess what? I have feelings too, not just you
Stop making me feel like I don't have the right to be mad
Anything I feel is supposed to be swept into a bag and thrown into the depths of my subconscious

Nah, forget that it's time to be brutally honest
I hate this. I'm not going to sit here and continue this mental abuse
You may not realize it, but you do
Talking at me and not to me
But let me say it's not always about what you do
I won't apologize for putting myself first
Doing everything I can to keep away the hurt
I write so you can feel these words
Always been cautious of what I say and how I move
All so that I continue to please you
Staying true 'til I'm blue in the face
Suffocated by your hovering and constant interrogation
Stop apologizing for not wanting to fall back in time, revert to a me that has been tucked away
I did so much for everyone else, I lost myself
So, no. I won't apologize for living my life.
It's okay, promise it won't be much longer
I've grown fonder of the desire to spread my wings,
Cause I've been like a caterpillar trapped in a cocoon
Break away from what no longer draws me in
On my own quest for the pursuit of happiness
Why do I always feel the need to say I'm sorry.
I'm really not.
Stop apologizing for being a new version of me
Sorry you don't get it, but it's not up to me to fix it.

WILL I EVER?

Will I ever be enough?
Now don't get me wrong I always loved me skin
Love my melanin and this dark brown afro
But I wonder will I ever be enough?
I went through school trying to fit in... or so they think
Cause really I was standing out, debunking the stereotype and living my best life
Followed all the right paths and listened to all the right teachers
I ran track at a white high school, so I always felt I had to prove myself.
Became a team captain and had to make myself small & say please with everything.
They said I was "The Hulk" because I asserted myself
But why is my strong personality so intimidating?
Why is my position not enough for you to listen?
I made it through high school with a 4.0 GPA, got into my dream school
And I soon had to face the world
I walked into college wondering was I enough?
Was I capable of doing the work that used to not be so hard?
Was I enough for those I needed to build connections with?
I'll graduate with a Bachelor's in Management
But, did I mention I'm a black woman
So will I be enough?
Because society taught me I gotta work twice as hard to be half as good.

Even though black women are the highest percent of college graduates and have a lifetime of experience, but we won't talk about that
I watched my mother work hard to climb the ladder to success
I listened to my daddy say I'm his little Oprah
But I wondered will I really be enough?
Am I enough for the Black man that sees me and doesn't speak?
Or the coworker who doesn't know what to say when my hairstyle changes?
Is my dark skin too much for you?
Is my power so strong you can't handle it?
Or is my confidence pouring out so much that I'll flatline before you can stitch it?
I stopped wondering if I'm enough because I know I am
I believe in me & everything I know I can be
I grew into the woman that can play spades with you and run an organization too
So will I ever be enough?
Let me put on my crown and see
Cause being a Queen…yeah that's enough for me.

TOXICITY

When the person you hang with, hangs with toxic people, how long do you think it'll take before you become toxic?
Before you start having regrets
Lack of explanations
And constant manipulations
It's easy to point fingers
But when do you realize your circle needs a healer?
Stop acting like a deer in headlights
Ready to put up a fight
But what are you fighting for?
Pushing everybody out the door
For what?
Don't let one situation
Destroy your reputation
I don't typically speak my mind
But through poetry it's my time
My time to speak what I see, even if it doesn't directly affect me
But it always does, because it affects those I love…
Yo circle is toxic
And I can't afford
for toxicity to enter my door
You not toxic…yet
And please don't let
Other's actions change you
Keep you from doing what you do
But I'm wise beyond that
I don't allow myself to get caught in a trap

I got a life of my own
I'm grown…thought you were too
But like Mr. T, I pity the fool
The fool who doesn't see fault in their actions
Creating distractions
A mental chemical so damaging
It's blinding everyone in sight
Poisoning the eyes of many
Having to wash away the toxicity
I say toxic humanity
Cause it's not just men with toxic energy
Yes women you too
The world don't just revolve around you.
Be honest with yourself
Do you need the help?
Look at your circle
And no these questions aren't rhetorical
Think about it, before you too, become toxic.

BLACK COUPLES

I'm Ms. Freeman
I got that 90s type vibe, in a 2000s world.
I'm a R&B type girl, in a time where music is City Girls.
My favorite movie is Love & Basketball,
My favorite song is Can You Stand the Rain,
And my favorite union is my parents.
I say this because I grew up watching black couples,
Balancing each other like a beam,
Radiating off each other's energy
Getting educated like DeWayne & Whitley
I want to support you like Michelle does Barack.
I want to laugh like we Martin & Gina.
I want to love you like Michael Kyle & Jay.
I want us to be successful like Jay & Bey.
And I want to stick togetha like James & Florida.
Let me be your Poetic Justice, freeing your thoughts and opening your heart
Putting things together like art
Let's make Love Jones
Building our aspirations
Reaching new destinations
So afraid to lose one another
That we take things a step further
And no it's not relationship goals, it's influence
Because everyone has issues behind closed doors, I'm used to it
Take the parts you like and create your own life
Making the decision to become your wife

Creating a home out of this house.
Building a family from having kids,
Not just sharing them cause they half his.
For me a strong foundation was inherent
And I see through it all like I'm transparent
For us to generate a life of love, we need to fit like a glove
And I know you'll leave me be
'til you know what you need
  Until then, we'll be here
    Living our lives
      'til the time is right
        For us to meet
         To introducing yourself like hi, it's me
       To locking eyes & knowing it's meant to be
  Now go
So you can grow
And we can glow
As a powerful black couple

GROWN-ish

You not grown, you're grown-ish
Because you still out here acting child-ish
Pointing out your age like it matters
But your mind also plays a big factor
The way you handle situations says a lot about you
Says a lot about your differentiation of business and personal issues.
I'm a woman so don't make me less than just cause you're a man
I need for everyone, let me correct myself, men
To stop telling me I can't think for myself
Oh cause everything you say is right, huh
Cause everything you do is right, huh
Cause your thoughts are what's right, huh?
Wrong
Baby, woman made you
We are the sole creators of the world
Stop putting us down and hushing us like you don't need us
Without us your world falls apart, then what
A whole bunch of brothas who don't know where to start
Almost 30 going on 13
Ready to be extra, make a scene
You may be grown-ish.
I'm tired of childish adults.
You claim you better than others
That the world you live in is how life works
But at what point do you realize, you are the backbone to all the drama

The reason people stop coming to a space
Women try hard to keep they private life private
'Til you mess them up so much they write about you and go public
But when it's time to confront a situation
You bypass us like it's nothin'
Funny to claim you man enough, but when it's time to be man enough, you ain't manning up.
Military don't mean nothin' when you still out here actin like my little cousin
Businessman playing mind games like Houdini
Acting like John Cena, you can't see me
I won't submit to your every word
And I'm not doing things your way everyday
So throw people under the bus, throw a tantrum
I got a mind like Thanos
Snap and you disappear
Cause there's no room for grown children here
See I've taken care of my fair share of kids
None of which are mine
So there's no reason to baby a man who don't even share my bloodline
And what's worse, it's the ones you never thought.
The one who you were cool with from the start
But you watched their ways unfold
Watch them have a stronghold over multiple lives
So much so when opinions vary, they think you picking a side
But don't even waste your breath
Stop feeling the need to prove your point
Trying to give answers to a man who don't need an explanation

I don't go back and forth with children
So if you want to be childish, by all means
But I can no longer have children on my team
When you ready to be grown let me know
Or just like a lot of others, you can go

SHINE

It is you that
makes me smile,
that's why it's hard
to let you go.

B & N

Standing in this library
Trying to figure out the words to say
I get so wrapped up in the energy
That all I can do is start typing and walk away

THE LION KING

This is a story about a Lion who claimed he was king
A man who claimed to protect the kingdom
But steady pushing everyone out of it
Slowly watching old people disappear
While constantly only cycling new peers
Look around you, whose still there?
No familiar face huh
No remnants of what was huh
The lion wants it that way
Wants you to forget who used to play
But look again...
They pop up every now and then
But what was it about the "king" that made them want to leave?
That made them feel they no longer wanted to be in the presence of this "king"
This Lion claimed he was a king
But don't disagree with the lion cause he'll kill you, kill your desire to continue coming back.
Coming back to a place you once thought was safe
But you'd rather avoid the bad energy & stale face
You think the rest of the jungle doesn't notice?
Notice that this lion no longer has a family
Abusing his power, using money as the reason
The money is making the man
Pointing it out like that's all the matters
Well without the jungle the money means nothing
Stop acting like the people don't mean something.

Constantly holding his ego so high like it's Simba on Pride Rock
He roars just loud enough to only hear himself
To only listen to his thoughts
So much so he makes himself a victim
Cries out like Scar so the people will believe him.
Forever tell the story that makes him wounded
Let me say this
He is not a victim.
He would just rather hold the grudges than get rid of 'em
He would rather push you away than learn from you
He would rather argue than be open to
Other reasoning.
A king should listen to his council
Rather than be doubtful of their loyalty
Lion you are not the only royalty.
Ask and we'll tell you about this lion,
Who claimed he was king, but turned out to be a man with no one left on his team

UNTITLED...FOREVER

I used to be so happy in this space
But it's a lot harder when there's no longer a familiar face
I used to just be
Smile and free
But with each day
That started to fade
Started to dissipate into thin air
Losing grip on what made my heart warm
Piece by piece, the peace that once was, is no longer
Used to make time for this like a retiree
But now there's other places we'd rather be
And I know from the outside looking in there seems to be no problem
Well from the inside the lack of respect is common
I saw you no longer saw my worth
I looked into the eyes of what I thought I knew
Realizing they were no longer there
So I left
It became the government
You know, the one surveilling my every move
A constant police officer watching everything I do
Like society doesn't do that enough... to this black woman
Like walking through the door is a crime
Like being the middle man is what I want to be
Like my words are fighting words
Like I'm an enemy
It's hard to feel welcome

It's hard to feel wanted
It's hard to feel…yourself
Making a home feel like a house
Making what was positive energy, a negative charge
But I know something better is beyond these walls
Cause as soon as I dipped off, better opportunities and blessings started to fall
My peace became better
My happiness got higher
My smile got brighter
So if you don't see me
Just know I'm doing better
I'm being better
And I'm giving more to someone who deserves it…myself

ROLLERCOASTER

When you were young the attendant would ask you to stand next to a bar to see if you were tall enough to ride.
Well what about the ride of life?
Would the moment you came out the womb be the guide?
What if you felt you didn't measure up no matter how hard you tried?

Nipsey said "Success or greatness come with a roller-coaster ride... anybody can apply the marathon concept to what they do."
Don't be scared
Get on that ride
Take that chance
Choose to be the best you that you can
To be that powerful woman, or impactful man.

Realize that the ups are slow and steady, but they are important
Because that's when you get the chance to observe the scenery
To see all that you can't from ground level
To know where sky's the limit and what you see is endless
So when that drop comes just know to look up
Look up to those that have made a difference
Choose to be fearless
And take the risks that will leave you speechless.
Persevere through the twists and turns
Using each one to learn
How to be a better you
Because one day you're gonna get off this ride

And when you do, I want you to look back and have a legacy that will outlive you.

ODE TO POETRY

Picking up the pen to write a poem
Is like picking up a bottle to get liquid courage
Picking up this phone to type a poem
Is like the adrenaline rush a runner gets when she's winning
Picking up these words off the page
Is like releasing the stories embedded in your mind

See poetry is an outlet,
It is an expression that needs no explanation
It's relative and up for interpretation.
See poetry allows me to express my thoughts in a way my mouth could never say
It lets me tell your story without everyone asking if it's mine
Poetry has allowed many opens doors
Poetry has let me have conversations I never thought would happen before
Poetry has given me an escape that no man can

Picking up the pen to write a poem
Is like picking up a bottle to get liquid courage
Give you the courage to pour out your life
Gives you a reason to fight
Fight for your mental health
Because much like generational wealth
If you don't create it
It'll bypass you,
Your mind is sacred.

Picking up this phone to type this poem
Is like the adrenaline rush a runner gets when she's winning
It lets me process this mind that keeps spinning
It keeps me from saying something I'll regret
It keeps me from having one too many anxiety attacks
It keeps me from falling back into depression
No anti-depressants, just public expression

Poetry has held most of my tears
Poetry is the home for my fears
Poetry is my fictional ear
Hearing all my thoughts
And poetry is the one place that I let my thoughts to get caught

MY ROCK

I get scared
Every time I look in your eyes
And fear that the mother I love
Is losing sight of her purpose
Losing sight of her happiness.
Trying to be the light in her darkness
Becoming the boulder
Protecting the pebble that has become her ego
Questioning everything as if somehow she's to blame
To grow to be like you is still my aim
See my rock can take on all things
Because all things work in your favor
So your strength will last forever
There's no words to describe what I see in you
I get a bird's eye view of the life you've established
And no, you aren't average
Don't think less of yourself based on the thoughts of everyone else
You are more than enough
You are the backbone to what makes me whole
My rock looks like it sunk into a hole
Worried that it will be stuck there
Not knowing that soon God will wipe your tears
And place you back on top where you belong
Knowing all along that you are meant to be
Meant to be everything you've dreamed to be
You ask if you've been a good mother

You've been the best to me and my brother
You created a good life for us stop wondering
Pondering on where things went wrong
You have strong-minded kids
It is what it is
I love you
But when I look at you, sometimes I worry
The biggest supporter you have
Is worried that you won't choose you
The biggest supporter you have will always hold you when you cry
Don't have to ask why
I am a part of you
So, the hurt you feel, I feel too
My rock has healing properties
It has spiritual abilities
My rock has a heart too
So, don't let the clouds of life overpower you
But rather let the rain cleanse you
So when the sun comes, your power shines through.

CHOOSE YOU

When do you decide to choose YOU?
When you're fed up and have had enough?
When you've cried all you can cry?
Or when you are at the point where you're all you have left?
When do you decide to choose YOU?
When everything around you is crumbling?
When people start belittling your achievements?
Or when no one's worried about you but you?
When do you decide to choose YOU?

HOW ABOUT when people stop seeing your worth?
HOW ABOUT when life starts bringing you lemons to make lemonade?
Or HOW ABOUT when you see everyone being toxic and you want to be better?

Choose YOU when you realize YOU are amazing.
Choose YOU when an opportunity comes that you CAN'T pass up
Choose YOU when you want to become something and prove people wrong.
Because,

Your HAPPINESS is what matters
Your PEACE is what matters
Your JOY is what matters
So choose you every chance you get.

3 WORDS

If I don't say "I love you"
Then we can remain surreal
If I don't say "I love you"
Then the pain of you walking away hurts less
If I don't say "I love you"
Then I can push down how I really feel
If I don't say "I love you"
Then I can neglect the thoughts I suppress
If I don't say "I need you"
Then I can act like I'm good without you
If I don't say "I need you"
Then we can avoid the effects on our mind
If I don't say "I need you"
Then I can keep to myself what is really true
If I don't say "I need you"
Then I can believe we'll last longer than time
If I don't say "I want you"
Then we'll go farther than our desires
If I don't say "I want you"
Then I wonder if you want me
If I don't say "I want you"
Then the rest stay serious inquires
If I don't say "I want you"
Then I can think you'll be a guarantee
But if I don't say anything
Then you'll walk away
And every part of me wants you to know
what I feel is real
Despite what I may not say

YOUR PRIVILEGE

You use your white privilege in black spaces, and you don't even realize it
Let me break it down and summarize it
Just cause we both black don't mean we get the same flack
Your privilege shows when things don't go your way
But there's nothing we can do for those to hear what WE say.
Maybe, one day, take yourself out of this box that passes every inspection
And become that box that gets every question
Yes, I'm black
No, I'm not foreign
Yes, I'm dark skin
No, my black is beautiful
Don't look this way and become overcritical
They say black people face colorism
I say it's all hypnotism because to say we battle the same things is a lie
Women are more incline to walk by that fine light-skin black guy
But clutch they purse around the brotha of a darker color
Become the dark skin black girl who has to justify her bun with TSA
Look at advertisements, chocolate kids becoming another PSA
When we look at TV, we always saw you
It's not until now that everyone gets to see our hue
In a better light than the overworked momma or a thief in the night
See being mixed with white has it perks
You get a privilege that society believes others don't deserve

And please don't be the face for me
Because to the world, all they see is you not me
Now I ain't saying don't fight for our rights
I'm saying add a lil more cocoa to your puffs if you're fighting for all our lives
Think about what it feels like for us
Your white chocolate may taste good
We are the dark chocolate they claim is bitter
We are devil's food cake I wonder why
You don't even realize that you are every other box of cake when we walk by
But it's because your white privilege shows in black spaces and you don't realize it
It's infused and can leave the rest accused and faulted for a life we didn't choose

NO MJ

Careful what you put in your body
They want you to believe it's better
"Oh it's natural, must be healthier"
Little do you know it's eating away
Eating away at your gums and affecting your lungs
Marijuana, weed, mary jane
No matter the word it's all the same
Deemed as an alternative
Supposedly making it the superlative
Constantly saying you did your research
Well research shows that they don't know
Unaware of its effect, cause someone hasn't died yet
Well death doesn't have to be the only impact
Handing it to patients like water
Freely allowing it to your sons and daughters
Giving someone an unsupported drug is not the answer
Just because it's not a cigarette doesn't mean it can't give you cancer
From someone who only smoked weed...
How is oral cancer the diagnosis she received?
A prognosis only handed out by your favorite woman
Mary Jane
Don't let society fool you
She can do damage too
Stop thinking you're above society.
Cause this, this is a story about my auntie.
Now I know somebody will negate me

Probably question, even hate me, but
Stop feeding into the bs and listen
Listen to the voice of experience
And no, it don't make a difference
No lace, no trace, no extra strand,
Just another item made straight from the land.
Sitting still, holding family's hand
MRI's showing you what they can
All in the middle of laying through a cat scan
Patiently waiting for the doctor to open the door
Watch his lips move as he says Stage 4.
Trying to remain calm felt more like a chore
Being told what to do
Since now, your life has a limit too
Taking in the radiation, eating away at her body
Having to receive chemo like it was a hobby.
Questioning how insane
Wasn't no tobacco just Mary Jane
Society keeps saying it's better
Well I hope you think twice after reading this letter.

MY GOD

My God
Is a healer of all pain
My God
Sees those tears and knows your fears

But my God can move mountains
He can do what no man could comprehend
He can hold you up when down is all you see
Dry tears when you can no longer see your destiny
You are fearfully & wonderfully made
Don't let no man let you think God has no plan
For your life

The One that gave me the courage to fight for a life that I was ready to give up on
The One who made me leave the confines of a hurting home
The One who at any hour will answer the phone

A spiritual lifeline that has no sense of time
He closed doors I thought were meant for me
Took me away from a lifestyle I believed was meant to be
Wipe tears to say thank you
You cannot control every hour
Sit back and let God show you His power
See God has a plan for my life
So today I pray, Lord make it right.

BEAUTY

A flower.
A piece of God's creation.
Strategically designed to see its changes.
Having the ability to protect itself
With the need to be watered to preserve its health.

A being.
Guided by light
Needing to be nourished day and night.
Trying to find the right patches in life to grow
Waiting in the wings to determine when to go
Such a beautiful sight to see

See beauty is like a flower.
Watch as it blooms and goes through stages
Every stage, breathtaking
Even the ones that are painstaking
Longing for attention
Wanting to be led in the right direction

MY ANXIETY

I've heard anxiety is a person's best friend
Well to me anxiety is more like a boyfriend

The one you love to have around when you want
But when he gets on your nerves, you want to walk away and be left alone
Make you think you can handle life cause you grown

You know, you just want your anxiety, I mean, him, to stop talking and listen
Paying way too much attention on what no one said

You don't want him playing with your emotions, but as soon as the game of life comes on, neglection is on the screen
And all you hear is screams

My anxiety is like that boyfriend no one wants you to have
The one who tries to control your thoughts
Make you think you're the problem
You know, the one you gonna cry over
But know they'll be back tomorrow

But's it's also the guy your whole family loves
The one that's there to get things done
Encourage all your triggers
Support your desire to be a quitter
Your boyfriend will let you have the greatest anxiety attack ever

This one completely loves you
So it's not like he'll ever really leave you
Right?

Cause he is your type
So the desire for him will never really go away
As soon as you think you're good
He'll just pop back up
So it's safe to say he'll be back…one day

OBLIVIOUS

You think I don't see you
No, hear me again
You think I don't SEE you
Watching your brain spin
When you can't get out everything you're thinkin'
Watching you tell me your thoughts
Afraid that if you let anyone else hear them, you'll get caught
Caught up in the doubts and what ifs
Provided by people that generate the 3 fifths
Or maybe it's from the 3/5ths that society said they wouldn't make it & they chose to claim it
So they project they misplaced hatred
Don't let negativity crowd your productivity

You think I don't see you
No, hear me one more time
You think I don't see YOU
Trying to hold back your every tear
As you sit around in fear
Fear of losing everything you worked for
Feeling like life is closing another door
Holding it all like carrying all your bags from the grocery store to the front door
Blind to the fact that someone always has your back
Ready to shield you from your demons & face every attack
Don't get so caught up in independency that you form a tendency to keep others away

Oblivious
become conscious
Conscious of your actions
Reassure your abilities
Keep a positive mentality
There will come your time
To radiate and shine
Despite the obstacles and curved life lines
And no matter what you do
I. See. You.

GIMME A MINUTE

Wow, that's crazy
The only thing I thought I was cool with
Turned out to be what I loved, then hated
My feelings and thoughts were always sacred
Opening up to the world
Well that wasn't your decision to make
Relinquishing the reigns
Only to put them in the hands of someone who let my heart break
Vulnerability,
Yeah next time I'll remember to hold that in
Because here lies a heart that I gotta mend.
But "don't be shady", "don't be petty"
But for how long can I let my heart sit heavy?
Heavy with the burden and thoughts of what if.
Refusing to resist and break the silence
Wish I was Raven, lemme be psychic
Cause if I knew then what I know now... issa no.
Stopped caring whether you were there
Diversions & aversions seemed to become a common trait we started to share
But there's always a part that still cares
So take the time to open up and let's clear the air.

THESE STRETCH MARKS

I stand in the mirror
Wondering if my skin could be clearer
Little girl wondering why
God gave her thighs with lines.
Doing everything I could to make those lines go away
Mom not knowing kids at school stay having something to say
Making this little black girl self-conscious in a space where she was already the only black face
It wasn't until I saw a brotha
With the same marks on his shoulda
Stretch marks
A representation
Of growing into something full of determination
These thighs carry lines to show you the growth and strength in my walk
On what's behind to show you I can sit at any table and I'm ready to talk
These stretch marks are my everchanging birthmark
I embrace them cause they're my personal art
I no longer stand in that mirror and criticize what I see
Cause when I stand in the mirror, I see me and every part is exactly how it needs to be

TUNNEL VISION

I don't know what it is
What is it that draws me to you?
A personality that pierces through my skin
Maybe it was the mind behind the melanin
Or the emittance of strength and confidence
Seemed like qualities that make sense
But I sit and wonder
Have I slipped further away from wanting your presence?
Or have I grown fonder?
You always give a sense of comfort
Like if I'm in your presence, I'm protected
Safeguarded from the world
A support system when life gets hectic
What is it?
What's keeping me from letting go?
Is it that little piece of hope or that part of me that glows?
A feeling not reciprocated
Making common conversation seem complicated
The unfortunate side of being one-track minded
No, you're not mine, and I'm not yours
But side eyes slide in like open doors
When I see you look to someone else
See having feelings like these don't help
At the end of the day, the only thing I can say is, welp
You not mine anyway but what about one day?
7 & a half hours, 7 & a half weeks
Time flying by and feels like eternity

But still when your name pops up I run back like an athlete
Gaining the same adrenaline rush as if this was a track meet
This can't continue
I keep trying to climb a wall I can't break through
Thought if I stopped talking for a day
These feelings would go away
Why is that not the case?
Maybe someone will fall in the mix
Change my mind and give me a new fix
But this tunnel vision might keep me from who I could be missing
Another soul understanding my issue
And all I could do is continue to wish it was you.
I don't know what it is
I wish I had the time to make a list
But I guess…it is what it is

THROUGH YOUR FINGERS

It wasn't until they slipped
      out of your hands
That you understood
      what their presence meant
You realized their grasp
      allowing them the chance to go free
Change the trajectory
      of the inconsistency placed in their path
You let her slip
      far away from you
And now there is nothing you can do.

It wasn't until you fell
      through the cracks of your heart
That you understood
      what pain felt like
You realized your dependency
      allowing mind games to alter your vision
Changing your perspective
      of what life was supposed to be
You let them release you
      letting go of negativity
And now you can be, completely free.

MIDDLE MAN

I don't play both sides
I'm a neutral stand by
See you act as if this is where I WANT to be
It's only because you both meant something to me
Funny, no one truly cares how I feel
How I 'm the one that's gotta deal, with everyone's mess
Did you ever stop to think, what about me?
See it's easy to tell me I'm picking a side
Solely because I didn't let everything you say ride.
I no longer bother to check on you cause why?
Why give you your time, when it was so easy for you to dispose of mine
Like all of a sudden what I say barely matters
What about after?
You say you stopped acting funny
But when I ask you a question, you start... acting funny
Silly man, I mean rabbit... tricks are for kids
I see through what you hid
Behind those words you didn't say
Because I read between the lines
And at the end of the day
You put me in a place I didn't choose to be,
and chose my consequences for me
So, I'll keep my distance & preserve my peace
Cause being in between YOUR problems isn't the place for me

THEY CAN'T MAKE ME HATE YOU

I grew up in Southeast
Now for those that don't know
That's the hood of Daygo
I've interacted with my fair share of officers
A lot of them had much to offer
I went to an elementary school
Where doing a program made being around cops cool
I had officers in my family to ask question to
Like why is it that you do whatever you do?
I've watched multiple simulations
And how they react to various situations
I have a different perspective
And no, this doesn't negate anyone else's narrative

But, no
I'm not sorry that I don't share your mentality
And yes I understand people have different realities
But to try to train me to look at police with distain is hard
I want my brother to come home, just like you
I want my father to live to see every day through
I get just as scared knowing what an officer could do

Black officer, I want the system to protect you
White officer, I hope you see the life in someone before you shoot
Hispanic officer, I wish they saw the worth in what you do
Because I know you want to go home too.

Despite the wide range of brutality portrayed by those in Blue
The world cannot make me hate you

I cannot hate when this career gave my family jobs
I cannot hate when the cop mentality is what helped find my brother in the middle of the night
I cannot hate when I experienced cops in a different light

Not all instances are negative
Sometimes listening is imperative
Create connections
To build and repair relations

Someone asked me one day, what was one word that I felt when it comes to police?
All I could say was divided
Because I see officers in multiple lights
But I want to see the men in my life come home at night

But, even in that thought,
Morning, Noon or PM
You cannot make me hate them
And even as I write this poem
I'm not worried about how that makes you feel

INVASION OF PRIVACY

You took everything from me
Watching me as I walked away
You had the audacity
To believe that what was mine, was yours to take
In that moment all I could do was cry
Cry away every memory, every picture, every thing
Don't tell me, everything happens for a reason
Not in the moment, my mind won't reason
I couldn't help but think, why me?
Why did you feel the need to target me?
Broke in and no amount of concern for my feelings
Shattered glass became shattered thoughts
Not knowing when I was going to feel any better
Pushing through day by day
Trying to come up with whatever words to say
When everything else around me was unstable
You became an earthquake
Shaking up everything that was solid
I felt safest in this car
I can't help but get scared, when you implanted a mental scar
To play back this memory
Is like creating a mental enemy
Your momentary exhilaration
Created a personal & mental invasion

Release Your Thoughts…
It's Time For Them to Get Caught

"The one way to get me to work my hardest, was to doubt me." – Michelle Obama

"Don't count the days, make the days count." – Muhammad Ali

"Surround yourself with only people who are going to lift you higher." – Oprah Winfrey

"Limits, like fear, is often an illusion." ~ Michael Jordan

"To achieve anything great in life you must be willing to make a sacrifice" – Kelly Rowland

"Decide to be happy... Smile today... A smile is a curve that sets everything straight." – Rev Run

"I am not my hair, I am not this skin, I am the soul that lives within" ~ India Arie

"If you can make it through the night, there's a brighter day"
- Tupac

"Confidence is built when you stop caring what other people think"
– Aiyana Freeman

"Life isn't how many breaths you take, but it's the moments that take your breath away." – Will Smith

"Black women aren't bitter, they're just tired of being expected to settle for less." – Issa Rae

"Do what you have to do, to do what you want to do."
– Denzel Washington

"The first time someone shows you who they are, believe them." – Maya Angelou

"For every person who doesn't like you, there's gonna be someone who does." – Lance Gross

"The most alluring thing a woman could have is confidence."
– Beyoncé

"Dedication sees dreams come true." – Kobe Bryant

"Cute accessories always help bring out your outfit and pull it all together." – Ciara

"I encourage women to just feel good about who you are."
– Anthony Hamilton

"Reflect on your past...look at your present...and think about your future. Is it where you want to be?" – Aiyana Freeman

"Wake up in the morning, say everything is outstanding"
- Leon Kearse a.k.a. Grandpa

www.ingramcontent.com/pod-product-compliance
Lightning Source LLC
Chambersburg PA
CBHW032055150426
43194CB00006B/541